# RACE AROUND THE WORLD

BY JEANNE MARIE FORD

MOMENTUM

Published by The Child's World®
1980 Lookout Drive • Mankato, MN 56003-1705
800-599-READ • www.childsworld.com

Photographs ©: Everett Collection/Newscom,
cover, 1; Da Liu/Shutterstock Images, 5; Everett
Historical/Shutterstock Images, 6, 18, 21, 26;
iStockphoto, 8, 15; akg-images/Newscom, 10;
IanDagnall Computing/Alamy, 12; Old Paper
Studios/Alamy, 16; Shutterstock Images, 22; Red
Line Editorial, 24, 28

ISBN 9781503832190
LCCN 2018962832

Printed in the United States of America
PA02421

# ABOUT THE AUTHOR

Jeanne Marie Ford is an Emmy-winning TV scriptwriter who holds a master
of fine arts degree in writing for children from Vermont College. She has
written numerous children's books and articles. Ford also teaches college
English. She lives in Maryland with her husband and two children.

# CONTENTS

MOMENTUM

# FAST FACTS

## Travel around the World

▶ Jules Verne published his novel *Around the World in 80 Days* in 1873. Its fictional hero, Phileas Fogg, traveled around the globe in 80 days. No real person had ever traveled around the world that quickly.

▶ During the race around the world in the late 1800s, airplanes did not yet exist, and cars had just been invented.

## Who Was in the Race?

▶ Newspaper reporter Nellie Bly of the *New York World* proposed to her editor that she would make the trip around the world by boat and train in 75 days. She set out from New Jersey on November 14, 1889.

▶ The editor of a competing magazine, the *Cosmopolitan*, read about Bly's upcoming trip. He asked **journalist** Elizabeth Bisland to travel around the world, too. Bisland had only six hours to prepare for her trip. Bisland left the same day as Bly and traveled in the opposite direction. For most of her journey, Bly had no idea Bisland was racing to beat her around the world.

**At the time Bly and Bisland began their race, ▶ people were not sure if traveling around the world in 80 days or less was possible.**

# CHAPTER ONE

# THE RACE IS ON

Nellie Bly sat in a chair held high by two men who carried her down the streets of Hong Kong in China. The homes on the hillsides gleamed white in the morning sun. The rocking motion reminded her of riding a horse as a girl in Pennsylvania. Bly felt like she was on top of the world. She had left the United States 39 days before and was more than halfway through her journey around the world.

At a shipping office, she tried to arrange the next leg of her trip to Japan. The agent in charge asked her name. When she told him, he said, "You are going to be beaten."[1]

Bly was confused. She was ahead of her planned schedule. She questioned the man more, and he asked her, "Aren't you having a race around the world?"[2]

◄ **Nellie Bly started her career in journalism in 1885 at the *Pittsburgh Dispatch*.**

▲ **Hong Kong was a bustling city in the 1900s.**

"Yes; quite right. I am running a race with [t]ime," Bly said.[3]

"Time? I don't think that's her name," the gentleman replied.[4]

"Her?" Bly repeated. The man was making no sense.[5]

"Yes, the other woman," he told her. "She is going to win. She left here three days ago."[6]

The agent told Bly she would have to wait five days before the next boat left for Japan. He felt sure that she would lose the race.

Bly couldn't believe her editor would arrange a race against another reporter without telling her. She tried to hide her embarrassment. "I promised my editor I would go around the world in 75 days," she said. "If I accomplish that, I will be satisfied. I am not racing with anyone."[7] But in her mind, she was determined. She would find a way to win.

## FEMALE JOURNALISTS

In 1880, about 98 percent of all reporters were men. Female journalists usually wrote about subjects such as recipes and clothes. Bly became famous for her daring **undercover** stories. Unlike Bly, Elizabeth Bisland was a writer of poetry, book reviews, and magazine articles. She had taught herself French so that she could read classic literature in its original language.

LE TOUR DU MONDE EN QUATRE-VINGTS JOURS

# CHAPTER TWO

# AROUND THE WORLD

One night in the fall of 1888, Bly went to bed with a bad headache. She tossed and turned, unable to fall asleep. Her mind wandered to thoughts of a vacation. Her uncle had traveled around the world long ago. The journey took him three years.

Bly thought about the fictional character Phileas Fogg in Jules Verne's popular novel. The character had traveled around the world in 80 days. Bly wondered whether it might be possible for her to make such a trip. The next morning, she gathered schedules for the city's ships and trains. She took a pen and mapped out a route and a plan.

Bly went to her editor, John Cockerill. "I want to go around the world in eighty days or less," she told him. "I think I can beat Phileas Fogg's record. May I try it?"[8]

◄ *Around the World in 80 Days* was written in French and translated to English.

▲ **Bly famously carried only one bag with her on her travels.**

They went to discuss the idea with the paper's business manager, George Turner. He declared that such a trip would be too dangerous and difficult for a young woman traveling alone.

"There is no use talking about it," he said. "No one but a man can do this."[9]

"Very well," Bly retorted. "Start the man, and I'll start the same day for some other newspaper and beat him."[10]

Turner finally promised that if the newspaper ever did use her story idea, she would be the one to do it. Nearly a year later, the newspaper's sales were dipping. Cockerill learned that a rival paper was planning to send a man around the world. He didn't want the competitor to gain readers over an idea that Bly had had first. In November 1889, he asked Bly to come to his office right away.

"Can you start around the world [the] day after tomorrow?" he asked her.[11] Bly smiled, excited for her journey to finally begin.

The next day was a whirlwind of activity. Bly visited a tailor to have a travel dress made. She needed a passport, money, and detailed travel plans. She would also need lots of luck during her travels. Any illness, weather delay, or mechanical problems could mean failure.

Early the next morning, she put on a plaid coat and cap and picked up a single small bag. She boarded a streetcar that took her to a ferry. It took her to her ship on the nearby New Jersey docks. A crowd gathered to see her off. She felt both excited and nervous.

On the ship, Bly thought about the approximately 28,000 miles (45,060 km) she would travel. She had never traveled by sea before. A friendly passenger asked Bly if she ever got seasick. Bly looked down at the waves. Her stomach began to churn as she thought about the long journey ahead of her.

A little while later, she took her seat at lunch beside the captain. As soon as the soup was set before her, she rushed to the deck and threw up. "The only way to conquer sea-sickness is by forcing one's self to eat," the captain advised when Bly came back to the table.[12] Bly was determined to make it through the meal even though she had to excuse herself several times. After lunch, she took to her bed and slept for almost a whole day.

## FASTER TRAVEL

In 1869, the Suez Canal in Egypt opened. It allowed ships to sail directly between Europe and Asia for the first time. In the United States, the **transcontinental** railroad was completed the same year. Finally, people could travel all the way around the world by train and boat. As travel became quicker and easier, Americans became more interested in exploring the wider world. Bly and Bisland used both of these new means of transportation as they raced each other around the globe.

▲ **Jules Verne wrote plays, short stories, and novels.**

When she woke, she felt better. Seven days later, she saw the shore of England.

A reporter told her that Jules Verne had heard that her trip was inspired by his novel. He wanted her to come and meet him at his home in France. Bly took two trains and a boat in the same day to reach Verne's town. He and his wife, Honorine, met her on the platform. Bly made an impression on Honorine. "She will beat your record," she told her husband in French. "I am so sure of that that I will **wager** with you if you like."[13]

"I would not like to risk my money," he replied, "because I feel sure, now that I have seen the young lady, that she has the character to do it."[14]

16

# CHAPTER THREE

# THE COSMOPOLITAN

O n November 14, 1889, as Bly set out for the New Jersey docks to catch her ship, Elizabeth Bisland had a leisurely breakfast in bed. She read her mail and the headlines of the day. She barely noted the news of Bly's race around the world.

At the same time, Bisland's publisher, John Brisben Walker, was on the ferry from New Jersey to the *Cosmopolitan*'s New York office. He read the front-page article in the *New York World* about Bly's journey.

Walker was an experienced traveler. He knew that at this time of year, Bly would be heading into the wind when she reached the South China Sea. He thought it would likely slow down her ship by several days. If he sent a reporter in the opposite direction around the world, he felt confident his reporter would finish first. He began to get excited about his idea.

◄ **Elizabeth Bisland was 28 years old when she started her trip.**

▲ **Both Bisland and Bly traveled on steamships.**

Surely the story of a competition would attract readers and boost the magazine's sales. He decided to place a large bet against the *New York World*'s publisher that his reporter would win the race.

Walker sent a messenger to Bisland. He asked whether she might leave that evening for a trip around the world. Bisland thought he must be joking. She soon realized he wasn't. Bisland immediately declined the assignment. She said that she had never been out of the country, she didn't own the right clothes for travel, and she had 50 guests coming over for tea the next day.

Walker finally convinced her. Bisland packed a trunk and two bags. A horse-drawn cab arrived to take her to a train station. By six o'clock that evening, she was on a train steaming toward Chicago, Illinois.

As Bisland traveled through western New York state, she was hungry and homesick. She wished she had never agreed to make this trip. However, as she saw Midwestern landscapes out her window, she began to warm to the idea. The rising sun shone on frosty fields. The sky was pure turquoise. "A perfect day," she wrote in her notebook.[15]

When she reached Omaha, Nebraska, she learned that a train carrying mail was about to leave for San Francisco, California. It was trying to make the trip ten hours faster than any train ever had. She got permission to board. When the train reached the mountains, the conductor picked up speed. The train lurched downhill. The passengers held tight to their **berths**.

The car lifted partly into the air. They felt as though they'd barely escaped death, but the train arrived on time.

On November 19, Bisland reached San Francisco. Two days later, she boarded a ship bound for Asia. Chinese immigrants on board, who were returning to China, released tiny scraps of paper into the air as the ship departed. Each contained a prayer for a safe voyage.

Bisland soon realized they would need those prayers. She lay in bed as a storm tossed the ship. Her belongings slid back and forth across the floor. The churning Pacific Ocean seemed to glow green through the **porthole**. She counted the wooden slats above her head to distract herself from thoughts of sinking into the ocean's depths. Finally, the storm passed. Bisland made her way back up to the deck. She was amazed by the sight of the open ocean. "The blue deepens and deepens," she wrote, "until one finds no words to express" its beauty.[16]

**During the building of the transcontinental railroad, ▶ dynamite was used to blast through mountains. The railroad made travel much faster for people who wanted to go across the United States.**

# CHAPTER FOUR

# THE WINNER

In December, Bly and Bisland sailed in opposite directions through the warm South China Sea. Bisland watched in delight as colorful fish darted beneath the surface of crystal-clear waters. When she reached Hong Kong, she met her first serious delay. There was a broken propeller on the ship she was supposed to board. She quickly made arrangements to take another one. It was slower, but left three days sooner. If she met her next ship in France on time, Bisland would land in New York ahead of Bly.

After eight days at sea, Bisland's ship docked in Italy. She sent a telegram to her editor to tell him she had arrived. He concluded that she and Bly would likely reach New York on the same day. A difference of a few hours could very well decide the race.

Bisland then boarded a train bound for France. When she arrived at the station outside Paris, France, a man greeted her.

◄ **Telegraph operators used a machine to tap out telegram messages.**

He identified himself as a travel agent from a well-known company. He told her that he had bad news. She had missed the ship. She would have to find another one to take her to the United States. Weeks later, Bisland would learn that the mysterious man was lying. She never found out why.

Meanwhile, Bly had boarded the same ship that had just carried Bisland from San Francisco to Asia. When storms struck, Bly despaired. "If I fail, I will never return to New York," she told the ship's officers.[17] The storms cleared. The ship arrived in San Francisco one day early.

## BLY'S ROUTE AROUND THE WORLD

1. Leaves from New Jersey
2. London, England
3. Amiens, France
4. Brindisi, Italy
5. Port Said, Egypt
6. Aden, Yemen
7. Colombo, Sri Lanka
8. Penang, Malaysia
9. Singapore
10. Hong Kong
11. Yokohama, Japan
12. San Francisco, California
13. Chicago, Illinois
14. Logansport, Indiana
15. Columbus, Ohio
16. Pittsburgh, Pennsylvania
17. Arrives in New Jersey

After more than 18,000 miles (29,000 km) of travel, Bly faced her first major problem. Snow drifts of up to 60 feet (18 m) had closed the railroads in the West. She was stuck.

The *New York World* had promised its readers that Bly's trip would involve only normal types of travel available to everyone. But the editors had too much at stake for Bly to lose now. They arranged for a special train to take Bly south around the snow. On January 2, 1890, she boarded a train bound for home.

Now that she was on land, Bly could receive news again. She learned that Bisland was on a ship from England that had been slowed by record storms on the Atlantic Ocean. Bly began to taste victory.

The *New York World* was holding a contest for the reader who could come closest to guessing Bly's return time. The paper gained hundreds of thousands of readers during her travels. Now, large crowds gathered at every train stop, even in the middle of the night. They brought gifts. Bands played songs written just for her. Bly was no longer just writing a story. She had *become* the story.

On January 25, 1890, Bly's train rolled into Jersey City, New Jersey. People crowded into the station to greet her. The official timekeepers noted that she had made her trip in 72 days, six hours, 11 minutes, and 14 seconds.

# CHAPTER FIVE

# AFTER THE RACE

On January 30, 1890, Bisland's ship sailed past the towering Statue of Liberty and into New York Harbor. Bisland's sister, Molly, was among the few people who greeted her. "She has beaten you," Molly said through tears, "but you did well."[18] Bisland's trip had taken five days longer than Bly's. Her return was barely covered by newspapers. "It is the winner who wins," one reporter wrote.[19] However, Bly's editors were accused of tricking Bisland into thinking she'd missed her ship in France. There was no proof, but some people claimed Bisland should have been the fair winner.

While Bisland's essays about her trip were published as a book, she never spoke of the journey again. She turned her back on fame and moved to England. She married a lawyer and worked as a writer for the rest of her life.

◄ **The Statue of Liberty has been in the United States since 1885. It was a gift from France.**

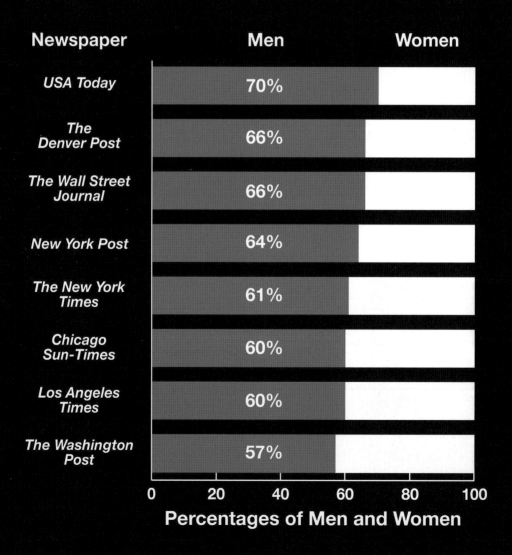

# WOMEN IN JOURNALISM

Bly and Bisland worked in a male-dominated field as reporters. In 2017, more men still worked in print journalism than women.

| Newspaper | Men | Women |
|---|---|---|
| USA Today | 70% | |
| The Denver Post | 66% | |
| The Wall Street Journal | 66% | |
| New York Post | 64% | |
| The New York Times | 61% | |
| Chicago Sun-Times | 60% | |
| Los Angeles Times | 60% | |
| The Washington Post | 57% | |

0    20    40    60    80    100

**Percentages of Men and Women**

Bly basked in the attention she received from the race. Babies and pets were named after her. There were Nellie Bly board games, dolls, and dresses. Bly was eager to return to writing. Her book about her travels became a best seller. However, she soon realized that she was too famous to work as an undercover reporter again. She left her newspaper job.

Almost 25 years passed before Bly resumed the work she loved. She reported from Europe during World War I (1914–1918). When she returned to New York, she wrote a newspaper **column** that invited readers to help others in need. Long after she died in 1922, Nellie Bly was remembered for her groundbreaking stories and, most of all, for her trip around the world.

## THINK ABOUT IT

► Why do you think so many people were interested in Bly and Bisland's trip around the world?
► How do you think Bly and Bisland have inspired today's female journalists?
► Do you think it's important that news outlets have an equal number of male and female reporters? Why or why not?

# GLOSSARY

**berths (BURTHZ):** Berths are beds on ships or trains. Seasick passengers on ships often stayed in their berths for days.

**column (KAH-luhm):** A column is a regular feature that a journalist writes for a newspaper. Bly wrote a popular newspaper column.

**journalist (JUR-nuh-list):** A journalist is a reporter who can write for television, magazines, newspapers, or radio. Bisland was a journalist for a magazine.

**porthole (PORT-hohl):** A porthole is a small window on a ship. A porthole allows travelers to see the ocean from below the deck.

**transcontinental (trans-kahn-tuh-NEN-tuhl):** Transcontinental means stretching across a continent. The transcontinental railroad made travel across the United States fast and easy.

**undercover (uhn-dur-KUHV-ur):** Undercover work is done secretly, often in disguise. Bly's undercover work made her famous as a reporter.

**wager (WAY-jur):** A wager is a bet. Jules Verne did not want to wager against Bly.

# SOURCE NOTES

1. Nellie Bly. *Around the World in Seventy-Two Days.* Charles River Editors, 2015. Print.

2. Ibid.

3. Ibid.

4. Ibid.

5. Ibid.

6. Ibid.

7. Ibid.

8. Nellie Bly. *Around the World in Seventy-Two Days and Other Writings.* New York, NY: Penguin Books, 2014. Print. 146.

9. Nellie Bly. A*round the World in Seventy-Two Days.* Charles River Editors, 2015. Print.

10. Ibid.

11. Matthew Goodman. *Eighty Days: Nellie Bly and Elizabeth Bisland's History-Making Race around the World.* New York, NY: Ballantine Books, 2013. Print. 79.

12. Nellie Bly. *Around the World in Seventy-Two Days.* Charles River Editors, 2015. Print.

13. Matthew Goodman. *Eighty Days: Nellie Bly and Elizabeth Bisland's History-Making Race around the World.* New York, NY: Ballantine Books, 2013. Print. 129.

14. Ibid. 129.

15. Ibid. 99–100.

16. Ibid. 149.

17. Ibid. 261.

18. Ibid. 321.

19. Ibid. 323.

# TO LEARN MORE

## BOOKS

Buckley, James, Jr. *Who Was Jules Verne?*
New York, NY: Grosset & Dunlap, 2016.

Castaldo, Nancy F. *The Race around the World.*
New York, NY: Random House, 2015.

Mahoney, Ellen Voelckers. *Nellie Bly and Investigative Journalism for Kids.* Chicago, IL: Chicago Review Press, 2015.

## WEBSITES

Visit our website for links about the race around the world:
**childsworld.com/links**

*Note to Parents, Teachers, and Librarians: We routinely verify our Web links to make sure they are safe and active sites. So encourage your readers to check them out!*

# INDEX